Edwardsville by Heart
Kọ́lá Túbọ̀sún

G000089277

"This book is an artistic map disguised
Túbọ̀sún is a poet deeply concerned wi
people, places, and moments in just the right spots on the map. Having
navigated a multitude of terrains from Ìbàdàn, Nigeria to Edwardsville,
Illinois, and beyond, he understands the imperative of charting pathways
and providing directions. *Edwardsville by Heart* gives us ways to get from
here to there and back again through verse. He becomes our guide and
fellow traveller as we traverse these important poetic recollections."

Howard Rambsy II, Professor of English,
Southern Illinois University Edwardsville

"This is an unfazed Nigerian linguist's exploration of some parts of the
United States of America where he encountered love and danger and
history. The poet-linguist reveals that 'I know nothing but tales told/By
winners and losers in a journey that began/In the effluvia of these river
banks.' There is talk of acceptance and suspicion in one breath. A music
of investigation and strangerhood. A tonality 'That welcomed sinner and
saints'.

"In form and content, this is a convincing collection of travel verse
tinged with nostalgia. I enjoyed the empathy, hilarity, and curiosity of
these poems."

Uche Nduka, author of *Ijele*.

"Like all of the great poets and travellers, Kọ́lá Túbọ̀sún gives us fresh
eyes to see what we thought was familiar, allows us to contemplate what
it means to be a stranger, what it means to belong, what it means to learn
and to teach, to listen and to speak. I love these poems for their textures,
for their palette, for the ways they map people and places, allow us to
consider 'what mark[s] us different, them and us,' allow us to consider
our intersections, the real and metaphorical roads that, like 157, '[go]
everywhere.' I love these portraits, adoring and searing, and the voices of
these poems, by turns playful and sharp. I love the way this book
reminds me of the transformative effect of 'words as shield or shawl.' I
don't walk out the same front door anymore having read this book —
now my Edwardsville is also *Edwardsville by Heart*, and my world is much
richer because of that."

Geoff Schmidt, author of *Out of Time*

"Kọ́lá Túbọ̀sún, in *Edwardsville by Heart*, brilliantly and attentively paints
an inclusive sense of encounter with a new place and a different people
through perspectives which are at once inquisitorial and acquiescent,
with uncommon tenderness and insight, amplifying in the process the
wonder and transmutability of the experience of human connection with
foreignness and difference. Túbọ̀sún excels in the art of subtlety."

Peter Akinlabi, author of *Iconography*

"The collection takes us through intricate travel paths, and each stop has a stimulating story to its antiquity. His vehicle of metaphors makes the journey a delight... every destination with varied colours of its historic burden. Yet in these journeys of discoveries, quests and far flung answers, there is a stunning crux, transforming complex issues into sensory, breathtaking images and music, with an authentic and electric voice. I consider Túbọ̀sún one of the best contemporary Nigerian poets."

Unoma Azuah, Professor of Creative Writing
and Writing Instructor at the Illinois Institute of Art

"The nomadic drive of this book propels the reader through the exploration of self as home, as nation, as language, as love and as displacement. With a linguistic flavour uniquely Yorùbá but played through English, we explore the many levels of identity, not to reconcile or even synthesise, but to understand that in the end, the self is not essential in nature, it is syncretic. As in all Yorùbá ritual, it is the journey that holds it together. You will not be disappointed."

Chris Abani, author of *Graceland* and *Sanctificum*

Edwardsville
by Heart

Kọ́lá Túbọ̀sún

wisdom's bottom press

First published 2018 by Wisdom's Bottom Press
Second (corrected) impression 2019

Wisdom's Bottom Press
15 King's Road, St Leonards-on-Sea, TN37 6EA

e-mail: wisdoms.bottom@zoho.com
www: https://judemontague.wixsite.com/wisdomsbottom

ISBN   978-0-9935502-3-2

Printed and bound by imprintdigital.com, Upton Pyne, Exeter

Contents

PREFACE

Once, at Oak Ridge Cemetery in Springfield, Illinois, where Abraham Lincoln is buried, Rudolph G. Wilson, stood and pointed: "Here," he said, "when I last came with a few scholars from Nigeria, your professor Rèmí Rájí[1] broke down and sobbed for minutes. It was all too much for him to take in."

Papa Rudy, as he was often called by friends, colleagues, and admirers, often dropped anecdotes like this into the middle of conversations. Often they were lighthearted and mischievous, intended to stir a conversation or argument. This time, he had intended to highlight the intensity of the feeling of history we had all shared after having walked through the vault where the assassinated sixteenth president lay buried. His memory of a similar experience many years earlier only validated what we had felt but didn't yet have words for. Yet what else struck me was that nowhere in that event was any sort of incongruity: not in the fact that Professor Rájí was Yorùbá, with ancestors who had probably never been enslaved, nor that the person telling the story, himself a descendant of African-Americans, perfectly understood why this breaking down in tears would have been a totally normal and commensurate reaction.

That trip to Springfield, one of many we undertook, usually in his S-Class Benz, around places of significance in the American Midwest while I lived in Edwardsville as a Fulbright Scholar in 2009 and later a graduate student from 2010 to 2012, has stuck in my memory for its unique tenderness. Then a seventy-five-year-old retiree from Southern Illinois University Edwardsville, Rudy had become a sort of human institution around Edwardsville. Deeply passionate about storytelling, about the African-American experience, and about connections across human, racial, and national boundaries, he travelled to give talks in nearby colleges, usually for free or for a small honorarium. Whenever he thought we would benefit from being there, he would invite us along, Máfòyà (a graduate student from the Republic of Benin) and me.

We had gone with him to Cahokia Mounds, to learn about the ancient Native-American settlement which had once had a population larger than London at the same period, and then was fairly quickly abandoned. He had also taken us to visit African-American exhibitions in Carbondale and St Louis and, at another time, to Principia to share stories about his life with students at the college there. At Col. Benjamin Stevenson's House in downtown Edwardsville, he worked as a storyteller performing one man shows and rôle-play improvisations about characters in African-American history. We were, to him, like young adoptive sons as he was to us a charming, yet mischievous, grandfather from whom we could learn

---

[1]Adérèmí Rájí-Oyèládé, sometimes referred to as Rèmí Rájí Oyèládé; a Nigerian poet and academic who taught me at the University of Ìbàdàn as an undergraduate.

so much. He was after all, the first African-American to teach in an all-white school – Claremont Grad. School, in 1965 – and the first African-American member of the Edwardsville School Board, of which he was later elected president. I had met him for the first time in Ìbàdàn in 2002 when he was visiting with a team of exchange researchers from Southern Illinois University Edwardsville .

His life in Edwardsville was not always rosy. When he moved his family to Gerber Road in about 1969, the neighbours there did everything to let him know he was not welcome, including leaving leaflets on which snide remarks about his ethnicity had been printed. His wife, LaVernn, had to change the locks a number of times. In the early seventies, when he was appointed by S.I.U.E. School of Education to mentor student teachers at Granite City High School, the folks there made it very clear to him that he was not wanted simply because he was black. Luckily, he had the backing of the university, which decided to stop sending anyone to the school until they accepted whoever was sent, regardless of race. The impasse lasted for over a decade, until 1991 when this unwritten policy of racial discrimination concerning student teachers was broken. This sort of incident defined his early days in Edwardsville, a town that now wears the character of a free, open, and tolerant community, and which would be my home for three years, and a distant adoptive home for many years thereafter.

This, and more, was my Edwardsville.

I've spent some time reading up on how the town has evolved over the years, and some of the rôles it has played, sometimes inadvertently, in American history. In an old courthouse in downtown Edwardsville, Lincoln was said to have made a few appearances as a young lawyer., and a few blocks away was another house where he was said to have stayed for at least a night during his first election campaign.

It was a speech he gave during that visit in 1858 that has retained a fascinating relevance. Edwardsville at the time, like most other cities close to the South, was sympathetic to slavery though not so fervently as to embrace it as fully as did its southern neighbours. Instead, it had 'pseudo slavery' laws, called Black Codes, which put several obstacles in the way of the "emigration of free negroes" to the state, and limited the rights of African-Americans in other significant ways. By the time Lincoln came to campaign, opinions were already divided on whether the abolition of slavery was a cause worth supporting. His now famous House Divided speech, first tried out before an audience at the Republican County Convention on the 18th May 1858 in Edwardsville, included the following lines:

> I believe the government cannot endure permanently half slave and half free... I do not expect the Union to be dissolved. I do not expect the house to fall; but I do expect it will cease to be divided. It will become all one thing or all the other. Either the opponents of slavery will arrest the further spread of it, and put it in course of ultimate

extinction; or its advocates will push it forward till it shall become alike lawful in all the States, old as well as new.[2]

It was a balancing act designed to bring along those whose votes Lincoln needed to win his then senatorial election without alienating their indecisiveness on the crucial question, but it was also an effective rhetorical strategy to illustrate the problem of slavery as an existential crisis with significant implications for the moral fabric of the country.

At around the same time, far away in Abéókuta – a West African city about 120km north of the Atlantic Ocean and 89km south-west of Ìbàdàn, where I was born – a different alignment was taking place. Cities and towns that had years earlier fought wars of annihilation, conquest, and enslavement, had started to consider the possibilities of truce, facilitated by force by the emerging colonial government from Britain. But in the early 1800s when the winds against slavery in the United States had started to blow, slave raiding and similar crimes against fellow residents of the area had only intensified. Warriors came from places as far away as Dahomey to attack coastal and inland towns, looking for able-bodied men and women whom they then promptly enslaved. *Clotilda,* the last slave ship to bring captives to the United States, landed in mid-1860 carrying over a hundred enslaved Africans.

Three years later, Captain Meriwether Lewis and Second Lieutenant William Clark were embarking from St Louis on an expedition to discover what lay within the wild virgin lands west of the Mississippi, which the country had just purchased from France. Although the aim of the expedition was to explore, map, and understand the new territory before other powers (especially Britain) tried to claim it, one of the outcomes was the colonisation and eventual displacement of the many Native American tribes, the taking of their land, and the destruction of their ways of life. In Africa, similar but larger expeditions were being conducted successfully, followed by the signing of similar agreements with non-English-speaking native authorities, small kingdoms, and emerging cities all around the region. This eventually led to the emergence of new countries, one of which is mine, Nigeria, officially created[3] from two disparate parts in 1914. Encountering the many human and material connections to these histories over many generations, and over many iterations of humanity across distances, becomes an animating impetus for this work, as well as the intimate familiarity

---

[2]This particular phrasing of the argument was later repeated on the 16th June 1858 at the Illinois State Capitol in Springfield, when he accepted the Republican Party nomination as a U.S. Senator. He lost that election, but the sentiment would launch him into the national limelight. It is today, along with the Gettysburg Address and his second inaugural, one of his best-known speeches. Quotation taken from *Collected Works of Abraham Lincoln*, Volume 2, pp 452–453.

[3]The technical word used is 'amalgamated'.

of the stories across race, nationality, and language. The challenges of humanity, laid bare in the intimate familiarity of these stories across skin colour, race, nationality, or language, is a more compelling motive.

Looking back at my time in that quiet part of Illinois and surrounding areas, through my encounter with the many human and material connections to these histories over many generations, from the classroom to the streets, is the primary motivation for this collection. Here I have sought to recollect an intensely affecting time, and to reconstruct utopia from the contrast that the period provides to today's news of a different and changing society. Since I began the Fulbright experience in 2009, I have kept a blog at KTravula.com as a way to document my thoughts about and experience of America as a scholar and teacher. But the spontaneous nature of blogging and the less than permanent nature of on-line publication nudged me to a more enduring, perhaps also further reaching, medium: hence what you now hold.

When I volunteered as an adult literacy teacher at the International Institute of St Louis in the Autumn of 2011, the number of new refugees into the United States the previous year had been 73,311[4]. Many of the adult literacy students I taught there came from places like Bhutan, Nepal, Somalia, Iraq, Cuba, and Burma, among other places of conflict around the world. The joy of watching these full-grown adults learn to read and write in another language for the first time, free of threats to their lives, and the privilege of being part of the process, is indescribable. Even though they looked different and spoke different languages, the students were intimately relatable. They were like my grandparents in Ìjẹ̀bú, my parents and neighbours in faraway Ìbàdàn, the market men and women I encountered in Bódìjà on my way to school, and the women who sold ẹ̀kọ and èkuru to us in Àkóbò. Most of them would eventually learn to read and write in English, pass citizenship classes, and go on to make a living as productive Americans. In 2018, the number of refugees admitted into the country so far is 5,225, a 65.8% drop from the first three months of 2016[5]. It has become a different country.

From Lagos, I have looked back at times with nostalgia. Yet it is very possible that my memories are tinged with a kind of privilege as well. Yes, no one called me *nigger* while walking on the street, or squirted cold water at me through plastic toy pistols from a moving vehicle, both of which had once happened to my wife growing up in Minnesota. I was a scholar on a government scholarship (later a University assistantship). There are tough parts of growing up American that were never going to be accessible to me. So, imagining the whole country as embodying the idyllic sense of calm that characterised Edwardsville while I lived there could seem like an unrealistic recollection. As you will find within the lines of

---

[4]Source: Pew Global

[5]Source: GlobalCitizen.org

these poems, I hope, the recollection was not always so rose-tinted. It is an homage to the times and to the people and places that made it memorable: friends, colleagues, students, lovers, mentors, and other acquaintances.

While he was in Ìbàdàn in 2002 for the scholar exchange, Papa Rudy had ventured into town in search of a real and unscripted African experience which the university, with its guided tours and arranged programmes, didn't always provide. He attended a church event at the invitation of an acquaintance, and had an experience he found horrifying. As he related it to me in his living room on Gerber Road, the priest there had made an altar call to "all mothers in the congregation" for some sort of benediction. All was fine and good until he also added, for effect: "all of you mothers who have carried children in your wombs."

For the American, most of whose children had been adopted, this involved an insensitive implication: that only women who had carried children 'in their wombs' were qualified to be called mothers. He was so upset about it that his voice rose when he retold the story to us, being sure to add how he went to the priest after the service to give him a piece of his mind. That was the Papa Rudy I knew and loved. Those were the stories with which we grew around him, and explored the complexity of the world, from one continent to the other, and from one generation to the other. Those were the things that highlighted the similarity of our humanity across different boundaries. Sometimes, we would sit down in his living room playing Tonk or Dominoes, or simply arguing about the difference in pronunciation of 'man' in Nigerian and American English — him making fun of our African accents, and us telling him we couldn't tell the difference between when he said 'man' and when he said 'men'. At other times, we would gather around the dinner table with his friends of many years listening to them tell the story of their time in the United States military.

On the 4th December 2017, faraway in Lagos, news reached me that we had lost him. He was eighty-two. In the Autumn of 2015, when I'd last seen him with my wife and son, whom he was meeting for the first time, the signs were already there of a coming end. He often fell down while walking around the house, and sometimes forgot things. But his warmth and passion had not waned a bit.

This work is dedicated to the memory of his generosity of spirit, curiosity and openness, and mischief. He represents for me the depth and complexity of the story of Edwardsville and the American Midwest, and a symbol of the benefit of travel for the expansion of empathy, knowledge, and imagination. I hope that this book serves as an artistic map of my lived experience for whoever else finds themselves in that part of America that holds so much personal and collective memory.

K.T.
Lagos, Nigeria
May 2018

I
VISITOR

Stepping Out
at Cougar Village

Outside, the trees
heaved yellow leaves
across the sky
towards the path from where,
stranger here, I paced
out into August,
feet to the brown earth
like divination fingers.

In the Fall, when the Village
wrapped its welcome
in aridity, the rustling of grass
welcomed with the honks
of the geese in the corners
flapping rage at strangers.

Behind me, the house from
where I had emerged faded
into one with all the others there;
colours of the season giving cover
to concrete homogeneity.

So memory returns
of the many demons from
which hope had sprung
that brought me here,
for which the journey
into this promise of a life
was some act of fleeing,
to which America
was both a saving grace
and distance, a respite
in shawl and shield.

To find my way
back into Apt 431 would task
memory and sight; tools
stuffed into backpacks from home
and years of wanderings
in the streets of Àkóbọ́ where seeds
of this present were first sown.

Campus Deer

No one would believe
that the African had not seen them
alive, this close, ever,
until language brought him there.

Certainly not the student who
regaled him with third-hand tales
he had heard and believed
of the Maasai outrunning a leopard
until it collapsed, too tired to move.

"I'm not Maasai," he should
have responded with a frown.
Instead, he explained the difference
between East and West, rural
and urban, Ìbàdàn and Rift Valley,
wide open lands and urban zoos,
village hunters and city dwellers.

At Cougar Village, the difference
was never exactly clear, which tickled him.
Brown friends on the lawn,
the animals ate behind the tennis court
on his way to class, and
stared at him with little interest.

Lagos–Ìbàdàn expressway, on poles,
hanging down the hunter's hands
like a roadside flag, their cousins
knew an African when they saw one
in the bush singing Ìjálá to the boom
of Dane rifles and waiting cauldrons,
pounded yam and fresh palm wine
ready to welcome hunter and game.

It was disrespect, he thought,
that venison could read, like students,
the signs that said: "Call 911
if you're ever attacked by a deer."

Peck Hall People

Here the friendly faces beat
my difference into company,
alien into friend, a feat –

Belinda, Catherine, Doug, Olga,
Tony, Heidy, Tom, Sherry, Joel
Kristine, Yvonne, Seran, Samba –

and a learner into a linguist
in three years, warts and all
with other moments missed.

The cleaner arrived on time
and greeted me in the morning
and then at night, a careful mime

of diligence that still moved me
though our words to each other
never grew beyond a short howdy.

In the day, students are spread
out on concrete, casually dressed
around the hall, faces like dread.

Sleepy marks on rosy cheeks
as questions of what becomes
of morning spent in moulds of geeks.

The F.L.L[6]. was home as much
as it could be, company and loves
gained in the fullness of its touch.

---

[6]Foreign Language Lab at the S.I.U.E. Foreign Language Dept.

At Tower Lake

I have one photo
of two lovers,
backs to the camera
on a Fall evening
with their faces
towards the grace
of Tower Lake.

The water lay
calming the scene
like new glasses
on a broken eye.
Around them the geese
fluttered with the ease
of cream petals.

The moment's promise
to a student's mind
spanned some seconds
that seemed to last
forever, with no words
to trap the lovebirds
into permanence.

So I rode away defeated;
my intrusion into the tryst
playing for my mind
like sweet prose
contrast to the rough
remains of the day
bearing the lovers' warmth.

The Preacher on Campus

In the square, he yelled at those who walked past
and strutted around to gaping crowds
on a break from Starbucks or a boring class.

They weren't violent towards him but stared
enough to give pretend thought to his words
with occasional yawns of those who cared.

He soldiered on with a zeal that moved
me from the distance of the circle, wondering
what pushed him there, what this passion proved.

In the cold, he cut a shape of a bloodied knight
daring the windmill of caffeinated youths
in what seemed a most unnerving kind of fight.

Meeting Rudy

Because fathers were to be found
not always in dusty record shops
in Ìbàdàn, or grandfathers sweaty
from a long trip from Àráró village,
home to celebrate the end of year
with thanksgiving at the Anglican
church down the street, palm wine
and yams, a new wife, bush meat,
and fruits from the year's harvest,
our meeting from over 400-year
gulfs poured itself into fully felt
warmth that lit up the evening.

We had met before, years earlier,
though he did not remember.
His photo albums kept the maps
of the past from where my restless youth
had poked its head through every part
of undergraduate impetuousness
at another mentor's tribute.

Tonight, far away from our first touch
in another homeland, his charm
(velvet for skin like the other grandpa
now gone into memory with the warmth
his visits brought in lightness across the yard,
or father now removed by circumstance,
growth and distance) beamed
towards my uncertain joy at his new offering:

The voice carried no hint of self-importance.
"You will need a bicycle to carry you around,"
he said, the town suddenly becoming smaller,
"and you can have this one."

Three Degrees Centigrade

When the touch of a student's hands
brought electric sparks to me
in December, I shrivelled at my coming fate.

Practice with a freezer back in Ìbàdàn,
trying out the state in which corpses rest,
provided no relief, then or now.

At Le Claire Festival by a glassy lake,
my hosts stared at my gloves in some
amusement, previewing what was yet to come.

Another time, towards the end of January,
Tower Lake, now frozen, called to curious feet
that wouldn't heed its ancestors' warnings.

"Winter lasts till March." The fluffy flakes
that fall on us by Christmas Day
returned no answers to tropical supplicants.

First Malaria

Six weeks in, I crashed down
in sweats and fever, with symptoms
all too familiar except to the doctor
and students to whom I could
only have been dying in instalments,
beyond American care.

With me, a few doses of home
calmed the room: Fansidar, Artesunat,
Paracetamol, as Nigerian doctors
prescribed. Not enough, though,
to calm the campus Red Cross,
to whom being Nigerian was enough
disqualification,[7] and would say no more.

Often, I remembered the joke
about the student from somewhere,
speaking British English, who answered
'drugs' when asked at the border
what he had in his luggage to declare.
He didn't make his next flight.

At Cougar Village, the mosquitoes
bore West Nile Virus and encephalitis,
and probed just as hungrily as the school
insurance administrators who gave no refunds
and no fucks, except the cold comfort that
it won't be just malaria that kills me here.

---

[7]As I realised that day, being Nigerian, having lived in Nigeria, or having had sex with a Nigerian, usually prevented one from being allowed to donate blood to the Red Cross. I wrote about that experience here: <http://www.ktravula.com/2009/12/the-blood-bank/>

Becoming American

Was easier than I'd thought at first.
Social Security number had arrived
a few weeks earlier, in an envelope
bearing little to assert its import.

Loving burgers was always a given.
A few years of suffering vain
cravings for mother's pepper spices
will eventually give the bun a chance.

A 'soup' here was not always a soup
with burning flavours on the tongue,
and 'yam' wasn't yam either; potatoes
and cocoyams posing around the plate.

Self-servicing gas stations took some
getting used to — as did the idea
that I could fill my car with fewer dollars
in Missouri, just forty minutes' drive away.

On South Grand, in a snack shop that sold
fried plantain chips and Nollywood movies,
I stopped to refill the stomach; at the counter
the Liberian lady asked if I used an E.B.T. card.

With people we can't greet as we pass
them by, we nod artfully with a hint of a smile.
With others we indulge in empty fillers
as they reveal spare facts about their day.

Cops are helpful when we're stranded,
as long as we let them pat us down first,
answering a list of queries about drugs
or possession of any types of weapon.

One time, a campus policeman came
to my rescue when car failed to start.
I didn't understand why I also needed
to sign indemnities against bodily harm.

On campus, the army recruiter beamed at me,
reciting his list of benefits for joining the military,
"happy to help" me escape a hell he believed
that my returning home could only mean.

"I'm a scholar here only," I said, well-prepared.
"It doesn't matter," his confident pitch
had clearly worked times before; not usually
met with "I'm not trying to become American!"

Sometimes, the country choked with a force
I could not recognise, a strangeness in the air,
a warmth that soothed and smothered
equally. Was that exceptionalism?

Being American in the Midwest is likely
not the same as elsewhere: the weather
for a start could qualify us as Londoners.
April tornadoes were a force of their own.

What is more American than travel? Staying
perhaps in one locale, oblivious sometimes
to local sites that guests from faraway
places visit in awe like houses of worship.

II
WANDERER

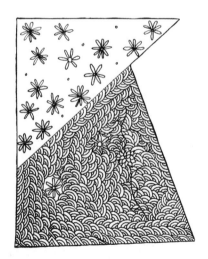

At Springer's Creek
with Olga and Nikita

At the edge of the evening are
conversations that charm the cold off
a newcomer's back.
The 1800 house on Route 66
to Chicago stands idly in the neck
of E's evening town, like a bracelet.

Red wine for the tongue, white for love.
Warm brushstrokes of the city's history
on the walls like sentries
stare with table lamps in warm-blood
hues of comfort, sate strangers to the music
of clinking glasses and bottles.

The kind lady offers us a taste
from the cask her wineries hauled
in names of generals and famous roads,
and we indulged.
Tasting is drinking, I thought,
and the Blush Table Wine
on our winter tongues seeped
like the warmth of young lovers
into permanence.

There is a band that often plays there,
sweet lullabies to our nostalgia,
strumming tales of long ago
into the current of our indifference.
Just don't call it 'lullaby' in a wine bar,
but beats and clarity. A warm pulse
for how to adopt a town.

Neighbourhoods

Edwardsville is four towns
or more: St Louis at a distance
to the south; Glen Carbon
even closer, with a lush embrace
of its rôle as twin sister.
The other two could be Alton
the quiet one, and East St Louis
in the naughty corner of dim lights.

But I can't be sure,
because the signs beside the road,
read from a fast-moving car,
point to different charms,
sometimes only in the sound
of their call: Granite City, Collinsville,
Maryville, St Charles, Wood River,
and other haunts carved out of the land
like cheese.

St Andrews Episcopal

Later, when I became a churchgoer
again – Papa Rudy's fault: father-friend
in a foreign land, offering comfort
with the warmth of winter heat –
the music and the coffee-hour snack
were an added boon to the company
of the curious people there.

The priest was a woman too,
helping the agnostic in me
out into acceptance of a different way,
out of the restraints
of a stiff Pentecostal past.

Rudy sang in the choir, and smiled at me
from a distance at communion
when the organ chimed in tune
with the Anglicanism of my youth;
lyrics like honey dipped in redemption.

At Christmas, the colours ran
with the warm whiteness of the town,
and love wrapped around our singing,
like a family bearing each other's cross.

Bike Paths

The city's belly opened up
when prodded, concrete veins
leading into where only a cyclist's
legs could reach.

So when I visited Holly
at Burns's Farm, off Franklin Ave.,
I was, in the cold, covered only
by the maps that my feet recalled.

Bikes cost only a few minutes
of grunt time, but spared
space for calm in a busied brain
the warrens recharged.

I explored when I could, alongside
joggers, city history drawn through
these lanes in stories unknown
to those who never looked.

Two wheels of Rudy's gift ground
through Delyte Morris on campus,
sometimes at two a.m. from Peck,
counting seconds with each muscle snap.

Going home to 431 in the winter
like a night ghoul with a backpack
through the school gardens, I bore the soft
sounds of crickets about my freezing ears.

Interstate 157

From a spot on campus
shortly after the last police car
from the St Louis exit to 270
I remember the speed demon
that rode on my shoulder
like a drunken toddler.

To the International Institute
and back, that spot always enticed
as the blind spot on cop radar
to recklessness
among the yellow brown
trees of the Midwest Fall.

Elsewhere, it took me to Ron's
on Forest Grove, or McDonald's
at the gas station near Bella Milano.
Wasn't there also a fine pizza shop
nearby, offering a rare evening view
of the summer sunset at nine?

She seemed around everywhere,
Interstate 157, from Walmart to Aldi,
linking downtown to Devon Court.
159 on the right towards Collinsville
was there as a choice on a bad day,
but the one five seven went everywhere.

Emergency Room
October 2009

The first visit to St Louis
was as an unlicensed driver.
A passenger with a broken ankle
on the other seat, in pain,
held the map in her shivering words.

Barnes Jewish was fifty minutes
into a town renowned with the worst
recall of the country's fears,[8]
beckoning the stranger's leaden feet
with frightened giddiness.

The curved bridges of highway exits,
wound sprightly like a bow
or listless belt upon the river,
were the first lessons in city plans
and E.R.s before Obamacare.

But the night ended well for the sick
and the stranger, bubbly in his happy
strike for impetuousness
against what he knew was risk:
"Nigerian caught breaking law. Deported."

The doctors were sure that the leg
wasn't broken but sprained,
strained like her pocket in the recession
and the shaky bones of the country
tethering on the many woes of '09.

Of what was the E.R., septic smell
around the hall, kids on one end
and broken adults on another, panic
in faces as roll calls to visitations held
back by new arrivals by gunshot.

To the stranger, familiar faces –
in U.C.H., Olúyoro, returned in colour, sister
on the operating table waiting for N.E.P.A.,
aunt just departed after an abscess –
only mapped out the country's pain.

---

[8]St Louis is often cited as the most dangerous city in the U.S.

20

I saw, in the night, tough garments
of the country weak, the battle with tears
and pain, face to face with more than just
A crowded room of poor compatriots, I wondered
what exactly marked us out as different.

East St Louis

I think they warned
that I might be kidnapped
or worse: "So stay away,
or take great care there
if you really have to go!" I heard
the city's name blaring red
everywhere, wearing statistics
and different shades of circumstance.

But E.B.R. lived there,
I thought. Redmond the poet
shuttled poetry from here,
black as Ethiopian coffee beans,
to Lagos and Ìbàdàn
in my undergraduate days, with
a smile on his oak-hued face,
a deep crack in the velvet
voice in which his verses rolled
into colours that rhymed
with grace, Civil Rights lore
in quartets of memory.

One day, with white
blonde classmate and brown
Moroccan scholar at a lit bar
near the river – Hollywood
it was called (and who cares why?) –
while topless girls on poles
smiling with extended tongues
wriggled glittered buttocks
to songs I'd never heard before,
I wondered where in these lights
the danger lurked.

On other days, we visit
the Community College Centre,
meet educators bearing
scars of lost time
in coarse voices across the hall,
in hands that sculpted brains
with charm and hospitality.
No dread there either
in their words or resolve
against the ignorance they
lanced with the patience
only teachers wield.

One day, at the spot
where the bus from Collinsville
joined the train that carried
passengers into St Louis,
a vagrant approached me
for weed, spoke in tongues
that flew over my head,
and not only because I was
also lost in the music that played
me away from the spot in denial.

Another time we got lost,
Máfòyà and I, at a wrong exit
from the highway, and found
ourselves where fear truly lived:
a ghost town near the end of time,
cracked concrete for roads,
laid between factory structures
that stood empty, wearing graffiti
for warmth, and weeping
it seemed, for a type of loss.

Home at Rudy's

Not red-nosed, though, Papa Rudy
in the fullness of his mirth still
warmed up a room to a glow

his heart taut like snare drums
that play loud joyfulness
thumped in full fluids of flair.

At Christmas, we ate till stupor
stunned the layers out of dread
from the pain of our student eyes.

Evening was chess and backgammon,
tonk and pesos on the kitchen table,
learning tricks from the sixties' streets.

And sometimes dominoes
with Máfòyà, talking trash with old men
to whom this was youth again.

There at Gerber Road, mirth spilled out
of our ears like happy tears
and home in the laughter of night.

At the International Institute[9]

"Give me your tired, your poor
your huddled masses yearning to breathe free".

Guide the new arrivals here, learning
to speak again like babes in a stranded tongue.

Give me the war-torn and weary
the tired hands drawing the cursive scrawl.

Bring your women with wrinkled smiles
to the day's lessons: learning the A-B-C.

Come, new nations in old blood, strangers,
scars and all, with slates at the English school.

We may make them ours, tongue first,
in the joy of what might be paradise

and share, from their eyes, the sweet relief
and comfort from their war-weary thirst.

But come, before the horde in rebel flags
take over the gates of our kindred hearts.

---

[9]The International Institute of St Louis is a non-profit educational and civics organisation whose mission includes helping immigrants and their families (many of whom have been relocated from war-torn countries) to settle in the U.S. and become productive citizens or residents through the learning of the English language, civics, and training for American citizenship exams.

One Two Three Seven

McClellan the columnist
was in the paper about twice
every week, journalling a critique
of the country in a way
that I'd seen nowhere else
and I wanted to meet him.

Bird feeders, squirrels
and robins, outside, came
to Diane's company at evening
while we sat on the deck
exchanging observations
of places we had lived.

The lemonade sold
in cans, frozen until emptied,
comforted my student tongue.
The cookies on the counter
competed with the spice
in the pantry the size of stores.

The clicker that let you in
to the garage where tools hung
and cat-litter sand
was mixed in bags with a shovel
felt like a nice toy
when I drove home from school.

The garden and sprinklers,
I remember, and the flowers,
with lawns we mowed when
the summer heat subsided
round the yard. No fence;
fences made bad neighbours.

A neighbour from Europe
and her husband swore that they
would relocate there soon.
I wonder what they knew was coming.
Others there were whose faces
I never saw unless I went outside.

There was Monty Python, and other
movies from antiquity
with dinner table conversations
of varied colours and flavours.
Stuffings, cookies, spice.
Irish, Nigerian, earth,
in several scents around the cellar.

We saw Real Time, usually
in real time, on Fridays
or on TiVo later if we went out
to Peel Wood Fired Pizza
where a long queue of hungry
customers shuffled round the place.

When I watched Fox News,
in the basement, sometimes,
I remembered to delete the proof
when I could, always,
to avoid explaining the craving
for angry blonde perspectives
on national life.

Study, cat litter, gym room
in the basement, and my room,
with a brown agbada on the wall
was either too hot or too cold
but the duvet, well spread
across my legs kept the cookies safe
underneath as I Skyped with Lóni
across the world.

BooBoo, the feline, woke
me up when we were alone
at home with an abrasive lick
across my brows, and mewed
requests from the foot of the bed
until I was up, staggering
towards his food bowl.

The artefacts on the walls
and shelves from Afghanistan
to Ìbàdàn to Milan to India,
Opon Ifá beaded cap, ram horns,
nested dolls, Kabul carpets,
ancient bones, pots, sèkèrè, often
provided comfort when, alone
in the large home, I sought
the company of memories.

Facing Westwards
at the Gateway Arch

With the river behind me, brown,
the noisy strength of its mystery
tumbling towards where they say is South,
I worried less about drowning
than the final deposit of my gangling flesh.

At St Louis, the Mississippi is the bridge
between histories, East and West,
past and present; a road to a history
now mired in soot, oil, sewage, and grime.
It wades along under the gambling boats
that skirt it like a common thief.

It's not memories that bring me here –
for I share little, except the humanity –
but curiosity. I know nothing but tales told
by winners and losers in the journeys that began
in the effluvia of these river banks.

From the Arch, the city spreads in white
shells into the far reaches of land,
casting stories, shadows across the face of what
once held a thousand secrets of a new country,
roughly taken, cut, hewn, and shot through;
like ears of wild wheat in a soldier's hands.

The Firepit at Karla's

I know where our youth most stirred
in the dry mist of Edwardsville nights
with wine on the tongue, and weed
in the evening to nostrils of campfire dogs.

I remember what marshmallows taste like
but not the s'mores: sugar-suffused crackers
you wrought out of burnt white fluff did not
always appeal to a tongue shrivelled by fright.

She said my accent got thicker by the hour,
by the deepening of night, the length of smokes,
the tide of drinks with which our friendships
tended open the secret we hid with prosody.

Like the kiss of a Swiss girl by the stairs,
or a tipsy look on your face, the chorus
into places I dared not acknowledge in company,
my Nigerian came out in the warm fire of night.

The bonfire sessions brought reggae jams,
Saki barking at movements outside the fence,
and fireworks blasting, that July fourth, at lines
that your country drew on the limits of liberty.

There was the doctor and his dame in ribaldry,
a chemistry of adulthood without care for rules
when delight would do, and a few drinks more.

Effingham

I'll remember this place
for the hilarity of its name,
censorship on the green road sign
that titillates the linguist's brain
to other effing possibilities
of the curious town.

With giggles for pleasures,
the entendre wrote itself
into the class examples I gave
with Jill playing along
in soft mischief. It struck me as strange
That it hadn't yet become a shrine.

"Maybe Fuckingham
was already taken," I thought

Mardi Gras in St Louis
February 2010

The beers in a can
were twice the cost

and turkey legs the size
of fat baby's thighs.

White boobs on balconies
appeared like gnome's heads

as the cold bored angry
moments into our bones.

By evening, our coloured beads
were spent on bosoms of delirium

and the parading crowd
appeared like masquerades.

Nothing there, though, was worth
the frostbites we happily never got.

I'd retell it to grandchildren as fancies
of February, whistling drunken songs.

Stagger Inn, Downtown

It was for the music that I came
but for the ravioli I returned.
The beers tasted of evening
like the glass clinks and smoke,
its bustle of bodies in the soft
glow of a summer night.

When the town is warm, the air
outside welds a wandering mind
to the thought of a melting pot
united by the strumming of guitars,
bluegrass on the stage, the right
to happiness in band harmony.

One barman like a bearded griot
spoke to me once through the nest
of his mouth, and made sense
of the world beyond what I'd judged
was the morality of a downtown bar;
the world was sane in that moment.

I returned often for comfort, or a view
of downtown reverie. Erato lay
across the road to the right, and the bus station
from Tóla's house. Straight ahead, the C.V.S.
sign glowed, where condoms were sold
alongside cough syrup.

Tornado[10]
April 2011

One Friday in the Maxima, I drove
in the rain, at night, for burgers
at McDonald's that cost about $10.

In the wheezing of the night
were light drops of rain, and warning,
in loud whirring of a strange sound.

"Light tornado alert tonight
at Edwardsville. Stay indoors please,
when you hear storm alerts!" a text said.

The road rattled with rain like drums,
with no warning bells of a coming doom
that only a stranger could ignore.

The hamburger came with bacon
and fries, and extra ketchup on the side,
with lemonade. For the road.

Whirring noises continued
away from the drive-through, with a warning
from the kind attendant: "Do stay safe, sir."

"It's not too bad, right? This noise," I asked,
displaying as little fright as possible
through the wailing siren. "I'll make it home?"

Only the rain replied in tough music,
rattling on the shield with stronger winds
than my wiper could swat away.

At Governor's Parkway, where 157 meets
East University Drive, was where
the turning span us into a whirl and dance

---

[10]A more devastating version of this event happened in St Louis
on the same night as this experience. By morning, scores of windows at
the St Louis Lambert Airport had been broken, cars had been flung into
people's homes, and many planes had been dislocated from their hangars.
The airport had to be closed for almost 24 hours. The tornado, rated EF4
at its strongest point with winds exceeding 165 mph, was said to have
been the strongest to hit St Louis since 1967.

like a weaver's loom to the roadside
in swirls towards signs warning of antelopes
and speed limits, a few times more.

The road took my drink, a giant-sized
cup, and with it my trust in stoic attendants
who never warned that the road was hungry.

III
TEACHER,
STUDENT

Class Sessions

My Yorùbá cap worn out loud
picked me out easy as a thumb
from any campus crowd.

I walked with it into class once
and silence swept the room
like a dozen breath-holding lungs.

Colour walks into indifference,
an African masquerade
garbed in flowing fragrance.

Curiosity saved us, them and me,
from the tedium of hour-long chats
as fun lectures for our reverie.

We made it up in songs and prose,
open minds helping the staving off
of our futile fears in overdose.

A Gourmet of Names

Once Trish and Amber and
Kurt and Sanders were beings
whose names – smooth on the tongue
like cookies in milk –
and Colby and Ronald, and Bobby
and Donald, hat-tipped to breeding
like fine European silk.

Teacher in a cap, bearing tonality
like moulds of àkàrà round the village
square with a rallying song,
I called to those who might join
to let their Americanness remain
for a while outside the class,
from Joplin to Des Moines.

So new folks can emerge
adorned like ritual initiates,
throwing off blandness for colour,
accents for tone, words sparring
on white tongues like spicy soup:
Abídèmí, Àjoké, Babátúndé, Olúgbénga,
Olúmúrewá, like genies appearing.

Being Yorùbá

How do you teach a state of being?
You don't. You teach instead tone,
do-re-mi like music on the tongue,
and greetings and norms; clothing,
and where caps bend on the head;
dance moves to restless beats that
skilled bàtá drummers replay
when you taunt them with
a semblance of competence.

How do you teach anything at all?
You don't, but you answer questions
when asked: of whether you had Six Flags
in Yo-ROO-ba-land or whether cars,
like those that belched fumes on American
roads with the rage of rebels
also plied ours. Or how we learnt
to speak in English! Impolite it was,
perhaps, to ask about huts.

So you play videos instead, Lágbájá
one day, and Kèlání another;
or books, *A Mouth Sweeter Than Salt*
to wake the mind to realities
in differently evolved places yonder
where plotlines of magic weave
layered ornaments into fabrics
of reality. And no, no *Thanksgiving*
in Nigeria either, except with kola nuts.

Phonology

Of minimal pairs,
Egbokhare had already
prepped the table of my
student's ready palate.

At English, the lessons
returned but with muffins
this time, helping down
the knots in our throats.

Hardman, Hildebrandt,
in cognates and data sets
surfed the waves of needed
theories with uncommon cool.

Discourse Analysis

Someone once warned me
of the cynicism that would now attend
the rest of my reading days.

Lines, she said I'd find, carried more than
the words they contained, the letters
they spread like loaves of deceit.

Gaps, silences, hesitations, reserves
said as much as yells and curses,
messages drawn in lines of open code.

And I saw it, when the politicians,
like skilled flautists charming a snake,
sprinkled words on crowds like magic tricks.

Midterms 2010

Snow days and midterms.
The radio blared ads alone
with music as pesky fillers.

Obama bad, Obamacare bad.
Death panels and government takeover
will kill grandma in her sleep.

Snow days and midterms
"If you don't like the weather here,
wait a few minutes" the locals say.

If the school closes, then it must
be bad. Grab apple cider and a warm
blanket across your legs

and dream of a fireplace with crackling
logs and wine and Louis Armstrong
booming: "What a Wonderful World".

House Parties

The Africans and all gathered
once in a while at Ike's house
or Abdiel's, or mine

to burn out the stress in music,
or other means of killing time:
Nicki Minaj, Katy Perry, Félá.

Away from the countries
from where we had come,
we gathered, a lost tribe.

I always wondered why
the ladies at the shop counters
asked for ID cards

before selling us wine,
as if the shades of our skin
somehow reduced our ages by half.

In the rowdy mess of youth
we found love and lust and cheer
in the arms of an alien place.

They say twenty children
cannot play for twenty years
so we did it, compact, in three.

Randleman

A walk across the field
that held the flagpole
in the middle of campus
was good exercise
unless it was for late payments
or a hold on class registration.
Randleman always remembered.

On the first days when
the lie of the land confused
the African's arrival brain
to compass points, I walked
through to Starbucks which lay
behind it by the parking lot.

A few weeks to graduation
the walks regained rigour —
with a grant here for research,
and a smile there, American in hue,
like warm cuddles of a place
struggling to let go, gently,
of its now disillusioned guest.

Graduation Day

A herd of vampires in a perp walk dance
and waltz to the Pomp and Circumstance.

In the stands, mother-in-law happily waved
at her new son with a joy she knew he craved.

On stage, when the time to get my handshake came,
I winced as the announcer murdered my name.

Jollof rice, puff puff, love, meat pies and all
had made it down from Minneapolis into the hall

to feed a horde from the town, readying a loss
as a gain, a dance for surrender to adult dross.

In the hall, the graduands share the last meal
of solace, in smiles that anxieties reveal.

Last Days at Cougar Village

Memories, it seems
are built like puzzles
on many layers of recall.

Bed emptied out and sheets
neatly folded away, I handed
my keys to the hall monitor.

Flight due in three days,
I bunked in a neighbour's room
grumpy from early eviction

but shaken for what remained
on the other side of the world
waiting with wide-open arms.

I wondered about bureaucracy
and the scholar dream of a wider
world of connected friends

across distances, making castles
of great causes; breaking ground
on which, sometimes, we might stand.

I had drunk deep in the expanse
of adventure, the breadth of curiosity
that surprisingly let me be

so this ending rendered contentment
moot, except for what remained to see
in hugs and goodbyes.

Reclined in the rented space of refuge,
the utopia of the coming days felt hollow
in the distress of limbo.

IV
PEOPLE,
PATTERNS

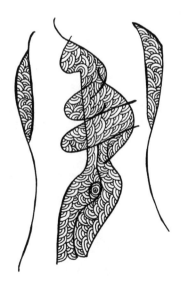

At Burns Farms
for Rowena McClinton

Gumbo shrimp gourmet on a table
spread near the patio where she worked
day and night, books around the room.

Mashed potatoes and gravy on another side,
greens, biscuits of the Southern kind,
greeted my palate in a structured dance.

In whatever language the evenings spoke,
a drawl from Mississippi and its charm
straddled her tongue like a warm stammer.

The Neighbour at Forest Grove

When I came out to get the mail
the neighbour did too, eager to talk.

"I've not seen you here before."
she said, like a fresh acquaintance.
"No," I replied. "I'm visiting Ron."

She was calm about it, an innocent chat
in the morning, between two strangers
at a neighbour's mailbox. Nothing fancy.

Except, by the time I was back
indoors, Ron had, faraway in Milan,
heard about the tall African in his home.

Country Mother
for Sandra LaVernn Wilson

You could find mother's love
in many places and flavours,
but she served it in collard greens,
dumplings, hot chicken wings,
and soul foods I newly met
when our youthful bellies cramped
into her kitchen at Easter time.

And more, of course,
since she kept Rudy active
through the decades of his mirth
and work and lore and restiveness
and jazz talk with loud laughter
the size of Michigan.

I don't know what Gerber Road
would have been without warmth
served like the ocean,
patient like a princess's smile
when we paced around the house
rowdy with mock impertinence.

I see her now, seated quietly
by the reading room, novel in hand,
and Joy in another, peeking out
to the cycle of feline time, wrapped
in the garden of flowers and masks
hanging on the many trees.

Panty Bomber
Mutallab Christmas, 2009

The driver's first request –
my feet in the school-bound bus –
was my thoughts on the Nigerian
whose attempt at heaven with a blast
through his sweaty pants
had rattled the country.

It had happened overnight.
We had heard in the news, too,
and my Nigerianness now lit me up
around the residence
as a hot voice in this winter ride.
Good morning, ma'am, it came. *I hope*
You slept well too in spite of everything.

We won't kill those not from our country
you know, unless they speak,
fluently, in one of our neighbour's tongues.
A true compatriot will destroy pipelines
before thinking of aeroplanes.
A slow roast from oil explosion fire
tastes much sweeter than an in-flight grill.

And, better to die in the fatherland
than risk another man's war.
No money is enough for a groin blast
unless it was bound to fail. 419, you see.
Al-Qaeda should have learnt never to trust
a Nigerian promised death for redemption.
Show him a queer neighbour to maim
for righteousness and that will do it.
Or the neck of a roadside thief to adorn
with a burning tyre.
No, ma'am, we would die for votes
come election time than for virgins in heaven —
those we'd get on earth by child marriage.
And cocaine will fit better in pants,
than bombs, in any case. Ask the masters
making hay with powders or princely stories
via e-mail across the world as you may have heard.
Are you sure he was a Nigerian?

But, when the words came, the eloquence
had withered with the weight of my name,
this far away, as the moment's national envoy.
"I'm Nigerian," I conceded, "but he's an idiot."

Driving with Ron

There's little that can be said
of the interstate that can be learnt
without being on it, speeding through,
two lives hanging in the balance
of one neophyte's mistakes.

So when I first drove with Ron,
from Missouri homewards,
it was to his credit
that he didn't eject me
for trying to hasten eternity.

His patience bred comfort
here and in the class,
where he dished Syntax like a meal
best served warm,
line by line in nested twigs
across the blackboard.

From Benin City to Kabul
the quick feet across the earth
hauled his frame like a mule,
hirsute, towards the moments
that gave him life: Emai,
Syntax, Diane, art, language.
Travel and, sometimes, me.

Cold Change

The black bus-driver
said my lack of change
should keep me in the winter cold
a few more minutes.

"You'll have to get down sir," she said,
my shivering foot on the doorstep
as the cold bore deep down into
the hollow of my African bones.

"Please", I protested,
twenty dollars outstretched
in a real supplication that feared the worst
from a sky that carried the frown
of an angry masquerade.

With the silence of our company –
a bus load of safe passengers
of many colours, bored
by this tenuous exchange,
eager for life in a warm city bus
away from the freezing air of a storm
now intruding with the strange accent
of the wheedling passenger –
I pressed my luck a little more
with a limp and a sigh; grocery bags slung
around my arms like excess limbs.

The blizzard gathered behind me
noisily in the coming dark,
but the driver maintained her stare,
as if nothing I said changed the condition
of a programmed response.
I thought she hated me.
My plea to stay in until the next stop
where I might find change
also failed to work a magic it would have
somewhere else – in Lagos – or with
a human at the wheel.

"No change, sir," repeated in a monotone,
ready to leave. "You'll have to get down."
Revving the bus for speed,
she rattled the controls of the creaky doors,
ready to snap my frame in two,
half into warmth
and half into the cold world
already scampering to safety.
"Now, sir", for emphasis.

Irish Mum
for Diane Schaefer

The day I told her
that I was driving to Joplin,
dreading the discouragement
of a doting mother
scared by the perils of the roads
or else the Maxima's ageing pains,

she said yes, quite easily,
with an added offer to help pack
my luggage with sleeping bags and all,
safekeeping tips about
what might cause the most problems
to a stranger in the country.

With Ron as the cautious dad
I smiled at my final adulthood,
free on the town on my own,
to put skills to test that once scared
even him on our driving lessons.

Months earlier, she had waited
with me on Troy Road at the D.M.V.
where I took my driving test and won
the right to drive the car
she thought I deserved to have.

"Let's see that again," she'd say
to Ron about a movie we'd brought
from off the shelves. "He'd like that."
And so, from *O Brother Where Art Thou*
to *The Life of Brian* to *The Holy Grail*
and *Fiddler on the Roof*, we laughed
bellyful into the merry night.

Irish mum, she loved
food and ribaldry, wine and spice,
books and Maher on TiVo,
and cats who licked my face at dawn
when they left us at home alone
with wooden gods around the shelves.

Sàngó at Peck

A Sàngó jacket on a bust
up at Peck, stares glumly
at me when I walk to class
on evenings when hunger
held my head in Syntax blues.

Its annotations often weave
proud affectation into my gait
in the box where its royal colours
glare as display gem for those
who cared that it was there.

But impotent, it stares at me again
through the glass on the day
after a tornado threatened
to throw me out of the country,
head first, without proper goodbyes
on Governor's Parkway.

Cold comfort to admire the grace
of a god I know so well, I thought,
lying helpless now against its rival's sway,
Zeus, over its resident town.

Ghouls of Convenience
at Lemp Mansion[11]

There are no ghosts gathered, alas,
in a haunted house waiting – as thought –
for us on Friday evening after class

With charred teeth and conical red
hats, black capes for night effect, or
noose in hand as the stories said.

My language had no word for such rites,
so I scoffed at what was said to be there,
crawling on ceilings in strange flights,

as the host and pamphlets wrote,
for a few dollars a head, deluxe,
on the bed where Charles self-shot.

The miseries live here, we were told,
and hung around still in empty moulds,
trading mischiefs that never got old,

earning royalties, making good hay
from curious guests from across the world
that sought spooky stories to take away

in tales invented for restlessness or cool,
the business of beer and the hospitality of fright.
We saw nothing but night in a drunken spool.

---

[11] A historical – but supposedly haunted – house in Benton Park,
St Louis, Missouri.

No Holy Land
for the Tamaris

Home, it seems, is not
just where the children are,
piano-skilled, courteous, all-American
like apple pie and sneakers
soaking Western culture into
identities formed many years
before trends and border lines
many times redrawn.

I have known your different home
or a lack of it, from the pain
of barricades, and disbandment
that citizenship of this New World
fails to erase or abate
when, at a border to the plots
from which your ancestors came
your Americanness meant nothing.

I have no answers for conflicts
or injustice borne with stoic resolve;
and neither did you, smiles and heart
at the table, in Edwardsville, hosting us
to hot food and love and laughter.
Reham, the Egyptian, likely knew better
what the alien years have meant
than I did, much to my shame.

There is no holy land, I will agree,
unless it is open to all that own it,
through blood and love and will,
and the stories told to keep it so.

Smokers in Glen Carbon

The cops never did stop by
to trace the source of weed smoke.

A twenty-one-year-old sister
of a friend knew where to get everything.

And wine never complained
as night companion to students' highs

on the patio, waltzing by like a dream
in December soothed by incense.

Youth met rebellion where none exists
and risks brought spice into our reverie.

When the Jamaican smoked, she saw a moon
where it never was, pointing from my window

and I wasn't sure if she had brought me there
to sing a different song, flesh to soft flesh.

When we spoke, the words fluttered
like brown leaves from tired trees

carrying nothing but doubt and longing,
to which we snoozed to promises never kept.

Youth is vain regrets, kisses botched,
vehicles wrecked in a love's fading dance,

hearts wasted on haunts of nothing more
than a chance to prove a need we didn't have.

Artist Colours
for H.R.[12]

She asked me not to write her
down as the lady in red
so I didn't, since the echoes
of that dress have faded into
the backyard of other lost causes

and what remained are shapes
of her, paintbrush in hand, wielding
the muse like an ankle pain
on the road, or places where the trading
of dreams kept an evening aloft.

Love was never supposed
to happen, so it didn't. The limits
of our dalliance spelt often only in
drinks in the hum of silence
with laughter and recall.

Her tennis shoes ran in circles
around the competition when they dared,
until overtaken by the pain
that depression brought with
colours like blood on the brush
present to fill where love used to be.

---

[12]Holly Watkins Ruff died on the 3rd January 2019 at the age of
fifty-two. Born on the 16th January 1967 in Jackson, Mississippi, she was
an accomplished artist and tennis player, and a dear friend, with a kind
and generous spirit.

Girlfriends

Cougar Village, in spite
of its name, was some type
of lover's paradise.

Behind my apartment,
a love bench sat and faced
out into the placid lake.

In the summer, the birds
fluttered on the face of the water
in glee and glamour.

One time, a lover and I
walked through the gardens
at night, and made love

to the sound of crickets
and silence and a cool breeze
around the concrete bench.

Graduate school love
came with its own variants
of circumstance.

One crush in class
and another within the group
of foreign acquaintances.

Sometimes, a weekend
was enough protection in the silence
of a lover's arms

with Nigerian food from Chicago,
a date at iHop nearby;
a love brewed to a six-hour distance.

And at others, a bicycle ride
to Burns Farms sated all bubbling
lust for thinking company

when all efforts with familiarity
in the space of campus opportunities
fail to rouse more than knowing hugs.

Shan the Caribbean stood out
with hair that ran through my hands
and a heart that held out through

summer entreaties, and driving lessons
in the alleyways around Franklin,
where neighbours growled in flaccid flags

at small infractions and noise.
She shared patois across the quiet
moments that our friendship allowed.

With the Indian, I plucked jasmine
in the spring to adorn her mane,
then feasted on chapati and mischief.

When Lóní came around
from Minnesota, we turned 1237
into the short-time nest of a new life.

Sometimes, loving warmed us
to parts of ourselves we never knew
or would rather have left unstirred.

Full Moon Winter

The girlfriend swore
that her soul flew whenever
the bright eyes of night
glared in the sky
like an orange bowl.

The blankness swarmed us
into longings, questions
from a sky that told nothing
but blood-blurry nods
to a place never forgotten.

Two Years More
for Lóní

Like yesterday's ripples on the Chicago Lake,
anxieties straddle our lips like the leaves of July.

Alone in the wind, we walked the busy streets
trading dreams with pedestrians and promises.

Long before eastern winds met Lagos dusts,
floating stories and floods in short moonscapes.

Long before chickenpox, and abduction, and Wúrà
rolled up trouser legs with other dawn daredevilries.

Bats, lizards, and geckos. I played commando
but you were no damsel in distress, fierce as fire.

Enticing evenings by the Lagoon, spice in the wine,
Nelson tugging with tiny claws at our night trysts.

To calm and daily renewals, clarity and other boons,
life, like soothing tea, in the right evening temperature.

We made it, didn't we? Moving block by block, as one,
or three — if the infant neighs count for something.

I will choose you again. Let's drive to Hannibal;
no longer hours away, but a destination of our tales.

Letter Home

Sometimes the freedom
from the worries that home
reflects back through broken
screens and voices present
in angry winds across time
frees the mind to pursuits
that pleased, that warmed
alienation into complacency.

But where is father now?
What new relapses of mind
can these texts from faraway
convey, a distance from childhood
where kindness cost nothing
and magic warmed through
every part of a breaking home?
What could distance heal?

I am here where tomorrow
begins with measured steps
as distress weaves into now
the past thought left behind.
A body craves rest where none,
dancing to hidden drums,
resides, where difference
deadens like a broken bell.

V
TRAVELLER

Home Alone, Traveller
at Cougar Village, 2009

The hum-dum of murmurs around a dirty rug
does not move, nor do the stirrings that tug
in whimpers at his idle mind, fall in random beats,
like hearts in a whirlwind of summer heat —
doses of silence, filtered in the glare in the evening eye.
"It will not be tonight the world ends." Only a cycle crawls by.
A darkening hovers around like an extra boring tale
from rivers to rivers, in bits of a least forgotten wail,
waving its sorrow, whining in old familiar tunes
sung many times before from grasslands to desert dunes.
This darkening, this solitude, this emptiness heaves
on a road often walked, littered with withered leaves.
I peer across a ledge, pondering time, pondering faces;
only a thick of quiet responds over a din of dank spaces.
It weaves a yarn of times, like a kind of cold, sour breath,
of stories told again to a non-listening ear; a certain death.
It is silent here as memory plays with the helm of choice;
"it will not be tonight that the world ends," in a quiet voice.

Finding Lovejoy[13]
at Alton National Cemetery

We had gone digging Lovejoy's climb
into public reckoning in a cemetery, tracking
the vestiges of his tumultuous time.

And that we did, stone by stone,
around land bearing history like a load
of sour fruits with seeds that won't atone.

He led the St Louis, and Alton Observer,
with views ahead of his time and hue
where hatred rode a sweeping fervour.

And he paid for it, bullets and drowning
a press in the pool, fire and fury,
an unmarked grave for self-reckoning

until exhumed and restored to grace
here at Alton and elsewhere, our library
at school bears him across its face.

Does he watch over this land at night,
his face on the eagle plinth astride the sky?
Does the river wash away history's spite?

We took in the sights, six of us from lands
where his name had never reached,
nor word of the deeds of his killers' hands.

Morocco, Jaouad; Benin Máfóyà, St Louis, Chris;
Yemen, Osama; Nigeria, me; and one more,
our fascinations, like ignorance and bliss.

We might have learnt something there,
though now I wonder if monuments do much
to teach except those open to their prayer.

Another name there tells of other ways to mourn:
"Vivian F. Schwallenstecker (1925–1928)",
tough to grasp like "baby shoes, never worn."

---

[13]Elijah Lovejoy (1802–1897) was a U.S. Presbyterian pastor, journalist, and abolitionist who was murdered for his work as an opponent of slavery.

A Springfield Surprise

I think I loved the capital
more for what it was not: remarkable.

The distance killed the flow of blood
to long legs stuffed in the back seat of Rudy's Benz,

and on arrival it seemed like nothing,
like bland winds on the face of Spring.

Lincoln was everywhere in name
from barber's shop to lumber mill.

We scorned what we thought of this
idolatry for tourists' delight.

Where he lay, at Oak Ridge Cemetery,
a Mecca of statue nose-rubbers fed

the myth of luck to those who seek it,
palms on the president's golden nose:

'Touch and be healed', the nose bore
all the tactile indignities with stoic grace.

The ghouls of his moral dimension flew
over our steps around the city, chasing stories

into the vault of his decayed flesh under
the slab, or the narrative of his immortality.

With another hundred pilgrims, we sought
a genie out of the Emancipator's bottle.

Lincoln in Edwardsville

The little house across from Tọ́lá's place
once hosted Great Abe in person, in 1858,
months into the fierceness of that race.

The words spoken there now have grown
better than the sum of our weary days,
contrasts to the bland corrosion of today's tone.

Signals to black coders and a moral rage
had planted soul in the soils of our quiet town.
I see him now, willowy, approaching the stage.

In sparse songs and dance, the lawyer
plays his thoughts across the bow of reason
daring Douglas into the corner of his cynic's fear.

At Gillespie's, the politician seeking glory
in the highest purpose must have weighed
pragmatism over meals with a charming story.

And later, by his stirring speech on Main
Street, by the courthouse there, he surely
helped to free a country from its poisoned chains.

I stared at it furtively one day in August by
the roadside, pondering the changes on the street
from the anamnesis of my mind's eye.

A free black man on Main Street in 1800
did not likely hold a camera 'phone, chasing history
down into another man's cottage free of dread.

And the street likely didn't lay spread out in tar,
a kneeling bus on one side of the road, with
gay men on the other, amorous beside the cars.

I peeked into what the past must have held, lines
in paint around the street. Railroads? Horses? Farmers?
Abolitionists and friends, with "Go Abe" signs?

And history beamed back hundreds in the rain.
seeking redemption of age-long sins couched
in laws of men, with blood and words for pain.

Are votes earned less by passion than by reason
and arguments for a better day and time?
Elections won without casualties of season?

The country may have survived it as one
but the man didn't, hole in the head by grief, pain,
and fear. It seemed that hate had won.

In Edwardsville, the chronicle had perhaps
lived but only in reverie. On the street here now is
nothing but the imagination filling the gaps.

Now on the barbed-wire fence: "Private property.
Do not trespass" sternly adorns the cottage,
humbly set, covertly, amongst the shrubbery.

Flight

Dawn wafts in from a distance —
a crimson glow amidst the cloud
like mounds of angry smoke.
We float above cumulus —
old empires wasting beneath
the loaves of precipitation.

The child in me always
believed that angels lived here
up in the shining layers of the sky.
Now, black hefts of crowded soot
hang there in shapes of gnomes.
Our wing extends into a distance —
man's reckless bet against wind
and gravity.

In this cubicle, this window view
into a waking world,
there is no silver lining, except us,
far above everyone else.

Defying the sky,
I am here as this daylight begins.

Destination Kansas

One day, four of us
packed into my Nissan
and sped westwards
in search of barbecue
and Kansas adventures.

Ikechukwu was the mirth
and dry jokes, Chris the ball
of angst and questions
and restlessness in the pleasure
of international company.

Abdiel was the muscle, leather
jacket with pick-up lines ready
in a Haitian frame that often
got the team in as much trouble
as it freed us from.

St Louis to Kansas City
took five hours in a straight
line of driving punctuated, sometimes,
by slight veerings onto the serrated
markings by the roadside

drawn to wake sleepy drivers –
me – when the strength of coffee
and conversations proved unable
to shake off the torpor
from insipid monotone sceneries.

At Fulton, we dropped by Westminster
to see Churchill, his statue
staring down the campus like a bully;
we walked through other moments too
in the shadow of his famous speech.

In Kansas, the World War Museum
lived up to its reputation. Life-sized moulds
of men sent to die for the empire
and other intentions in 1914
filled the rooms with many ghouls.

Africans were there too — from Burma
to other theatres where fathers and men
under the British boot laid down
lives to keep the powers free.
At least they live now on the walls.

From the Liberty Memorial, we
took in the sight of the city below,
concrete and industry, war and peace,
history in a space of private
remembrance.

The barbecue at Joe's would never
again suffice as witness, nor would a night
at a bar, seeking trouble and women,
and stories with which to remember
the last days, it seemed, of youth.

Chi-Town
2009

If no one has ever warned you,
hear it now: do not go to Chicago
in November – friends or not,
fun or not – however warm
the company, the colourful brand
of adventure that took us by bus
from St Louis at night, hearts
full of wine and endless mirth.

Do not go to Chicago in the cold;
it burrows into the bones before
you find the hands to throw
a shawl across your neck, plug
the drool of running fluid drawing
tributaries towards your chin
drying up above the other
in crusts of white, piercing dust.

Except for the pizza downtown
or the hostel near the lake,
where guests from different towns
had come, chasing stories, travellers
who, like us, slept on wooden bunks
and drank instant coffee when
the day broke, and we remained
just as poor as the day before.

Or the Bean, shining in the square
like a privileged toy in the sun.
Or Agora — headless brown sculptures
we stumbled on while walking around.
Or a photo on the ledge at Willis
daring us to trust the strength of glass.
Or the Art Institute with its hoard
of treasures from the world over.

Well, go if you must...
but not in November.

Visiting Joplin
June 2011

Six hours to Joplin
and five hours back,
I remembered the signs
on the highway, selling sex
to travellers at nearby motels,
and wondered to friends what
"the Bible Belt" meant.

A tornado took us there
and love brought us back,
four Nigerians in the Nissan
swapping tales of survival
the farthest we'd gone South,
chasing news and accents
with a missionary cover.

At Joplin, the wreck
spread over many streets with
mappings of violence like tribal
marks on a baby's face.
We had nothing with which we
could compare what we walked
through, helped through, but war.

I was never at Katrina,
though the stories Òṣúndáre
brought back in verse and wrinkled brows
echoed with a pain only survivors know.
At Joplin, we witnessed death
of circumstance, scars of succour
offering hands that were not enough.

Range Line Road, the centre spread
in the magazine of wet cosmic outrage
lay supine from the EF-5,
hapless with stories of courage
and misfortune: a boy snatched
from his father's now broken hands,
a pair transposed across the Earth.

"You loot we shoot", in spray paint
on a broken house, snarled in black
back at us on the field, where we moved
plank after plank, mending a land.
Langston Hughes, a native, once
spoke about a dream deferred.
And this was it, pall and more.

E.B.R. in Ìbàdàn
for Eugene B. Redmond, Poet Laureate of East St Louis

I thought I knew what poetry was
till music hit my face through well-sewn
lines that Eugene hauled along to Lagos.

Ewì always struck me as eternally
lost in the prosodies that English's
polished stanzas swallowed in slavery.

At Arts, and V.C.'s lodge, the almond nuts
he brought along cracked with the wisdom
of a connection of four-hundred-year dots.

And with Drumvoices, our verses sailed
into the seas, bearing rhythms of new colours,
staccato beats of what words once failed.

Sitting later at Starbucks at the M.U.C.,
we shared stories of those times, and faces,;
I drank in the largesse of his mystery.

Other Times at Alton

There are big refineries
at the sides of the road
breathing black carbon
into blue heaven's face.

"That's where Nigerian oil
lands first from the tankers,"
Ron once remarked to me;
"crude, before it becomes gold" —

It was also from Alton one noon,
when I saw on a ride back home
on the concrete walls of a bridge:
"Occupy Edwardsville" —
curious stirrings of revolution.

There is an Amtrak train that goes
to Chicago and St Louis from here,
gathering goodbyes and welcomes
of wayfarers into the early mornings
from our waving arms and hugs.

I remember the other school campus,
just a little, and the statue
of the Robert Wadlow, the giant, about whom
everyone thought that I should know.

There may have been others —
Fourth of July fireworks by the bridge
where the two rivers meet, we stared
at exploding skies of what Lisa said
was freedom.

Highland

Don't ask me about rednecks
because words matter too.
But when Karla took me home
to see the demolition derby
she used the word and I laughed along.

Her father had fought in wars,
and carried their stories like a gift,
with other souvenirs he kept:
swords, pistols, language.
I took to him to his daughter's surprise.

The derby was a waste:
tons of metal on wheels crushed
for crowds that once felt like a horde.
It took a while to find the second black
man in the crowd, towards the exit.

But the animals I remember:
chickens at one end of the village farm,
pigs at another, and bunnies.
The bulls walked with the grace of pets
not destined, at some point, for meat.

A New Year's Eve

From Erato Bar, pumped
with wine and mirth
at the coming hour,
four of us – a professor
and spouse, and two
foreign scholars from campus –
traipsed around town
singing "Auld Lang Syne".

Olga, the prof., also had cake
waiting for us at home
at one a.m., with leftovers
from earlier boisterousness.
At night, Edwardsville
on New Year's Eve, bubbled
out of a frozen human shell
into a colour riot of glee.

Principia

It was perhaps
Elsa that I remembered most,
that evil bird on the wall
facing a Mississippi that lay
to the left, supine like a rattlesnake.

But I also carry now
images of a curved drive up the hill
to the College where Papa Rudy
and Dr Afoláyan told stories of race
and reconciliation to rapt regard.

Ron spoke sometimes
about bird-watching trips
on winter days when time slowed
and humans flew like angels
into the arms of waiting heights.

Once, Shanique and I
drove around those streets for fun,
seeking paths out of normalcy
in a town surrounded by tedium.
I don't know if we learnt much else.

Three at Lewis & Clark

There's a memory I have, a dark
trace of three people walking
through a wooded swamp
behind the Lewis and Clark
College? Park? Memorial?

We were alone in the parking lot
and the premises were closed,
but walking around yielded
lots of treasures around the hot
afternoon, and we traded in boredom.

We had driven there with brave
Eloho and that one crush I had,
trying to kill idle time within
the wide shade the structures gave.
And that we did at the swamp.

It led, at one end, to a hill
with a spread of elephant grass
on either side, blowing cool air
as the wind tilted it to its will
through my legs. I was afraid.

It seemed strange that no-one
showed up to challenge us there, three
black people traipsing around
a government property in the sun.
And no one came for us in the foliage,

where we found coke bottles and other
proofs of life: a finished cigarette,
junk from careless folk who probably
came there, like us, in their
quest for peace, and maybe sex.

There was a wooden peg on the floor
at the back, near a log cabin
and, as I recall, I asked
when we could return for more,
when humans returned to roam the place.

But I don't remember much else —
how we got there, what we did,
or how we broke through the thick
air of the love that, later deemed false,
seemed to have hung from the trees.

Grapes of Recall

They most remind me of Edwardsville,
purple squirts of sweet, cold vagaries
of delirium in youth and nature's sugar.

The evenings across a flat plain
came with bloody sunset in the distance,
the wind blowing smooth on road 157.

The freedom on wheels satisfied,
one hand on the round flesh that soothed
the taste buds into fresh delight,

heat into calming A.C. breeze,
and music from a random station or N.P.R.
with that monotone of the world's fresh troubles.

The berries came like a collage of dreams,
the dry stalks and their unwashed seeds lay spread
across the Nissan's carpet, like sweet regrets.

Hannibal

By the Mississippi riverbank
two hours from my base
I stared out at what Mr Clemens
had seen, hated, or written about.

But it was also a date with a lover
who had come from the north
perhaps expecting more traditional
ideas of fun than a writer's village.

So we pretend-painted the white
picket fence of Tom Sawyer fame,
scrawling our names over other tourists'
in vain hopes of mortal permanence.

On the way back, we tried road head
at seventy miles an hour, glad for open
roads and sparse commuters who minded
their business, or honked for support.

We would return again three years later
as a couple, with our son, retracing steps
to where the dead writer's childhood home
had seduced another with open breaths.

Chi-Town II
2012

You mean more than evenings on Michigan Ave.,
sketched by paces in the breath of November dew.

Strangers we dared the night with wandering feet
into stores where laughter saved us from the windy streets.

Older tourists at the Lake rode on Segways when
they ploughed the ground, giddy like drunken men.

Ducks in the water, like the lazy boats, teased us
about what we thought we wanted from city flaws.

You mean more than trysts at —
days in the warm recess of your embrace, charmed

by the vibrant waters of the fountain, pitching glee
into the cauldron of its liquids throbbing for all to see.

You hold the secrets to evenings and loves lost
to distance, hearts poured in pages of stationery dust;

partings conditioned by indecision journeying down
Union Station and that college in the middle of town.

Bus rides to certitude, long train rides from Alton
and happy afternoons in clouds of a season.

Of Edgewater and the crabby streets of its nights,
far away in the safety of my bed, the thoughts excite

until run into by the sharp edges of facts, the allure
that love lost to distance may still long endure

but only in thoughts embalmed in parting words, fights
waged face to face, spoken on 'phones, whispered in the night.

Hugs of renewals, dates that would only be history,
second chances at capturing what may never be.

Shedd, Navy Pier, Grant's Park where guides could witness
the restlessness of our youth and nothing less.

This Chicago, this slice of dreams in its secret fold,
hides hearts in which stories remain, safe from the cold.

This Step, This Spot

And this is life, even as tomorrow crawls in with winks
or grim wings across an uncertain sky. Yes, this is the life
for which forerunners spoke, a day for which mothers' backs
broke with sweat and strain in odd colds of irksome strife...
It is now that beats the heart — two eyes across a dawning day,
and a flesh hung in space, with rasping sound of restless keys.
Here is where hope resides, not afar in the boxed, fuddled past
of rain on concrete cracks. It is not in the exile of many journeys.

This plinth of time must serve as totem to lit pathways
when the moon falls behind the hills, with a dry Western snore.
This step is new, but as of several æons and several memories
is old in the breadth of its pace, more than just a random chore.
I could ponder hope in alien lands, yet I shall not look behind
but inwards. In its charged spot are the loose moving thoughts,
each breath a treasury of lore, new paths bearing known marks:
I live in a ball of charms which dreams and hopes have wrought.

Edwardsville by Heart
for Mr Leicht

We dreamt of the South,
often, Chris and I;
a bus ride to the belly
of a past written of faces
and dusts and crops,
cops on horseback with batons
stalking the highways
in boots and their twangs.
We dreamt of many roads.

We would go to Memphis,
to Texas and Mississippi
in the Fall, we thought,
hand in hand on the streets
like lovers, in towns
where the fangs of history
wait on street corners
snarling at a love that
should not be, not show
itself capable of the excesses
of care and doubt.

We dreamt of the country
as a canvas of our youth,
a stretch for questions
of what the puzzles hide
in the tales we had been told
and in patterns that played
tricks on daring faces.
We planned adventures
into places which our curious
selves knew only in nightmares.

The road would offer us
succour from the rote of city chores,
streams of bicycle rides
into St Louis by the cycle lanes
drawn on the land like scars
that the old railroads left behind.
The South never came to us
but we warmed to the snaky
stretch of the tawdry interstate.

I hoarded toothless freedoms
from Nigeria, loud in sarcasms
that layered over the fears
peeking in often when,
at Lambert, a cop barked at me,
for leaving the car unattended:
"Can you read English?"
On Olive's, another politely asks:
"D'you know why I stopped you, sir?"
"No", but would I have told you if I had?

Up in Cahokia, in the mounds
that house the hill's dead secrets
steps marked on disturbed earth
were monuments to a once proud place.
The stories we heard, and the sights
we saw in stones and wax, warmed
ancient bonds to the pain of semblance.
At the head of chief's mound,
the view that stretched into the land
felt like lullabies to an American lost.

On the road, at a gas station store
where the blonde teen attendant stared
at me with mixed shades of uninterest,
we found Confederate flags for sale.
Many times later, in Kansas on a truck,
I found others, dangling in the wind.
At Barry, Illinois, I found the last one,
painted on the wall near where, stranded,
I had met the kindness of strangers.

At Hannibal we took in the history,
and the literature; at Kansas City haunts,
with the Haitian and Ike, like guards,
the sounds of an ancient war.
We stopped at Fulton to see Churchill
and his statue by the hall.
And at Cedar Rapids, we wept
with the Czech Villagers, and mourned
the wreck the floods had brought.

In fights, our passions rose
like febrile limbs; our points of view
rammed the other with lived
experiences; our idealisms
clashed with talking points
from the cauldron of cable news;
our differences played out subtly
like repressed lovers holding on
to something destined to last.

Recklessness stopped us eventually
at Clear Lake. The road ended
our approach to Minneapolis
with a crash I foolishly caused,
into the back of two cars travelling
from California with an elderly man.
My mistakes, sure, in the tedium
of road distractions with debates
about American exceptionalism.

"How's this for courage?" I joked,
stand-pissing on a tree at Iowa
in the front of the Capitol
with its gold glistening dome.
We weren't found or fined, yet
reams of the scare drawn taut
on the American's face
offered no response to the taunt
that this, indeed, was a freedom
that only my country allows.

Acknowledgements

I thank proofreaders, friends, and colleagues whose insight and support were helpful to the completion of this work: Chris Abani, Geoff Schmidt, Unoma Azuah, Peter Akinlabí, Uche Nduka, Yémisí Aríbisálà, Yémí Adésànyà, Howard Rambsy III, Máfòyà Dossoumon, Abby Ogunsanya, Chris Ogunlowo, Carole Oghuma, Chika Unigwe, Rópò Ewénlá, Títílopé Sónúgà, Precious Arinze, Stephanie Ohumu, and Benson Eluma. I thank Peter J. King especially for taking a chance on the work.

I also thank the families of the late Papa Rudy & Sandra LaVernn Wilson and Professor Ronald P. & Diane Schaefer, who made homes for me, Dr Michael Afoláyan and family, Prof. Rowena McClinton, Belinda Carstens-Wickham, Olga Bezhanova, Mariana Solares, Tom Lavallee, Heidy Cuervo, Rosanda Richards Ellsworth, Steve and Sandra Tamari, and Ajay & the late Jaye Lou Kansal, who gave warmth at crucial times. I thank Eugene B. Redmond, my professors Kristine Hildebrandt, Joel Hardman, Seran Aktuna; the International Institute of St Louis, the English Department at S.I.U.E., and the International Hospitality Program of the university for acceptance.

I thank the Fulbright Program and the Institute for International Education for the opportunity; and my friends, colleagues, and students, with whom some of these memories were made, occasionally in less flattering forms: Chris, Ikechukwu, Mohammed, Shanique, Eloho, Tómi, Abdiel, Chinomso, Asha, Abby, Leslie, Jason, Karla, Lisa, Iman, Tólá, Reham, Holly, Laura, Jill, Patricia, Luciene, Ronnie, Joshua, Yemí, Deolá, Aminat, and many more. I thank Emem Uko for the beautiful drawings she created.

I thank my parents, Chief Túbòsún and Elder Fúnmiláyò Oládàpò, for their sense of adventure, my in-laws Dr Francis and Mrs Grace Giwa for love and warmth, and my siblings Olápòsi, Omolará, Bukky, Yemí, Oláitán (1984–2016), and Adeolá for conversations and mischief.

Finally, to Tèmítópé Olúwalóní, my darling wife and anchor, for her presence and love, and to our son Eniafé whose presence enriches the desire for any long-term memory.

The poems "Home Alone, "Traveller", and "This Step, This Spot" were first published in 2009 on Ktravula.com and on AfricanWriter.com.